T0147681

JOURNEY TO ME

A Compilation of Poetic Works

Rachel Rechelle Craig

authorHOUSE®

AuthorHouse™
1663 Liberty Drive
Bloomington, IN 47403
www.authorhouse.com
Phone: 1-800-839-8640

First published by AuthorHouse   02/18/2012

ISBN: 978-1-4685-5621-6 (sc)
ISBN: 978-1-4685-5620-9 (ebk)

Library of Congress Control Number: 2012903311

Printed in the United States of America

Any people depicted in stock imagery provided by Thinkstock are models, and such images are being used for illustrative purposes only.
Certain stock imagery © Thinkstock.

This book is printed on acid-free paper.

CONTENTS

Section 1
The Foundation is laid

Section 2
Road to Heartbreak

Section 3
New Beginnings

Section 4
Same Endings

Section 5
Moving Forward

Section 6
Dedications to Friends and Loved Ones

For everyone who has ever inspired me to write.

"Sometimes you have to be your own cheerleader"

*F*ORWARD

As the friend I've grown to know Rachel Craig personally. From our close friendship I have learned that she has nothing close to a nonchalant or boring outlook on life. She's not your typical mid-twenties female. Her wheels are always turning and running faster than her feet will carry her. She is always diving into a new challenge, whether it is education, baking, and or writing poetry, which is her passion. Rachel's heart is bigger than anyone I've ever met and she is always helping out her family and friends; she'd probably give a stranger the shirt off her back if they needed it. Rachel has a talent that I envy, and the ability to throw her feelings onto paper in a way I wish I could. Her poetry is true and from the heart. She makes you feel her pain through the heartbreaks she expresses on paper. You will also find yourself crying tears of joy and pain as she shares some of her most intimate feelings with you. She speaks of love, heartache, and memories left from her past. Consider yourself privileged to read her work as you now have a piece of her heart. I've watched Rachel blossom into an amazing poet, mother, and friend throughout the years. I'm deeply honored to write this foreword for her. Rachel the sky is the limit and I'm so proud of you and the person you have become! You will always be my "Favorite Brown Girl".

REFACE

I decided to publish this book of poems because I felt the need to share my inner thoughts and feelings with the rest of the world. I know I am not the only one who has ever fallen in love or out of love for that matter. I believe that my topics are ones that many can relate to and find solace knowing they are not the only ones who have ever felt these kinds of feelings. A major contributing factor to the publication of my book is the constant nagging from my friends and co-workers about putting out a book. They are usually the first to read my poems and I have always looked to them for honest criticism. None has ever been given might I add. Either I'm that good or these people are not my friends, simply kidding. Whatever the case, it is my hope that everyone who picks up <u>Journey to Me</u> will enjoy it's content and be moved by it's sincerity.

ACKNOWLEDGEMENTS

I think it is only fitting that I acknowledge my loving parents Clifton Craig Jr. and Brenda Doles. These two people have helped to mold me into the individual that you will get acquainted with while reading this collection. Throughout each trial and triumph of my life they have been by my side, acting as guard rails every time I would sway to the left or the right. For their continuous love and support I owe them an endless amount of thanks. Mom and Dad I love you with all my heart and everything I do I do it for the both of you. It would not rest well with my soul if I didn't pay honor to the second most important woman in my life, my wonderful, educated, classy, dignified, Sister Amanda Craig. When I feel like I have no one else to turn to she is always there for me offering a listening ear and a word of encouragement. She will forever and always be an inspiration to me. For that Mandy I thank you. My other siblings Crystal, Matt, and Clifton you three are also near and dear to my heart and have added wisdom to my life more than you know. Love you guys as well. There are many other family members that I would love to acknowledge individually but for the sake of time and trees I will just add a line for you that express how much I love and appreciate your encouragement for me to live out my dreams. There aren't enough words for me to thank you. Tia I would like to say that you were a major inspiration to my poetry writing. I still have those very first poems we would write while sitting in 9th grade Biology class. It's no wonder I only got a B I was too busy writing poems instead of learning about the human cell. Never the less I love you best friend and I would not be who I am lyrically had I not got my start with you. Lastly I want to acknowledge someone who will never really understand or fully grasp the love that I have for them. When I didn't know who or what I wanted to be you came along and made my vision for myself very clear. You have proven to me that the desires of my heart can and will be mine. There isn't a day that goes by that I don't think of you and wish you well. Until the end of time you will go down as the one person that taught me how to love from the inside. If I never get a chance to tell you face to face I want to tell you right now in my first of many collections that I Love You and this book is in some way dedicated to you. If I have missed anyone charge it to my head and not my heart. I love you all individually and collectively and I thank you for taking the time to travel the uncharted roads of my heart.

Section 1

The Foundation is laid

ORIGINAL MODEL

Orbiting around in my own galaxy
I ride my magic carpet wherever it shall take me
Never weighed down by the harsher realities
Let my rose colored Blockers shade me
Some may call me shallow
Others say I'm nonchalant
Can't help I stay high without a blunt
Not easily moved by the trends
Don't surround myself with a lot of friends
Can't trust too many with information
Keep my guard up as not to be taken
From the surface my depth is not noticed
Never waiver from my path cause I'm too focused
This world can fool you if you let it
Think twice before acting so as not to regret it
Live like it's your last day on earth
Value true friendships you never know their worth
If you were to judge this book by its cover
You would probably put it down and pick up another
In essence this may be your biggest mistake
Might not think I'm real but I'm far from fake
I ride around on my magic carpet
Orbiting around my own sun
Can't find a duplicate there's only one

$\mathcal{N}$EITHER

Not quite White too shades too fair to be Black
Not considered a Sista cause it aint stacked in the back
My hair aint nappy and my lips aint big
Am I trying too hard when I try to rock a wig
They tell me my language is Caucasian
As if speech carries a certain persuasion
Speaking grammatically correct keeps me getting checked
I can't roll with the homies or hang with the crew
Not considered down cause I never rocked FUBU
Don't get it twisted they don't accept me either
When asked am I black or white I politely saw neither
Is it my fault genetics has my skin confused
I thought it was okay for people to come in different hues
Society needs to get a grip on reality
Slave master birthed enough niggas to form an army
My ancestors are a result of his tastes
Liked to pour his vanilla in chocolate milk shakes
So my grandmother was a bit White like me
It's because of her that I ended up with a flat booty
On the other hand her nigga fetish added a little color
To this caramel frape
Because of him my hips twist and sway
As you can see I don't fit into any category
My complexion helps to tell my story
I may not be as mocha as the sisters you know
But my skin is a little too dark to be an Eskimo

Proudly I walk around wearing my yellow tan
I'm not the child of a black or a white man
I stand before you representing a combination
To try and categorize me is like calling a Jamaican a Haitian

$\mathcal{D}$EAR JESUS

Grant my tongue the gift to bind
Don't hold me accountable for being blind
Ignore my inequities and defeats
Judge me not for being weak
Keep me covered in your blood
Love me simple because you said
You would

GOD'S LOVE

Simple arithmetic shows that one plus one equals two
For God so loved the world he sacrificed Jesus for me and you
The greatest act of love ever recorded
The gift of eternal life has been rewarded
For that promise alone our hopes should be high
We have a loving Father that sits beyond the sky
What he desires for us is magnificent and great
He made a vow to you and I that he refuses to break
God has a plan designed specifically with you in mind
All that he asks is that you be patient, gentle, and kind
Watch thy tongue and love thy neighbor
Through these acts sweet honey shall you savor
Be encouraged through your trials
Honor and respect God with the spirit of a child
For your efforts on Earth shall not go unrecognized
Even your troubles become a blessing in disguise
Through it all God should get the glory
Bless someone by telling them your story
Within each of us there lives a gift of ministry
Through love blessings shall be granted abundantly

My Three

First there was one then there were three
Never knew little people would be the beginning of me
I wasn't ready for your entrance into the world
When you came I was merely a naïve young girl
Life makes you grow up fast whether you're ready or not
I had to sacrifice for the three of you; I'm all you've got
Every day I strive to provide you with a life better than I had
It's a tough task when I want to run away so bad
The days get harder when I'm trying to do it on my own
But being a quitter is something my parents would not condone
So no matter how hard it gets and how bad I want to cry
I think about your innocence and the look in your eyes
You three are my babies and I love you with all my heart
You never have to worry about me leaving from you I shall never
Depart
I'm here till the end to love and care for you three
Through it all, it will be you plus me

$\mathcal{U}$NREAL

Why are you trying to pass off silver for platinum?
Cruising around in your friends Mercedes when you drive a magnum
Telling everybody you own the house you reside
Knowing damn well Wells Fargo told you the mortgage was denied
Can't keep your lights on cause you stay in the club
Screaming stacks on deck when you really only have a dub
Who really walks around in heels all day long?
Girl stop fronting after the club you didn't even go home
That's why you sitting at the Waffle House in the same outfit
Screaming you keep you it one hundred when your name aint legit
Same goes for these guys who claiming to be ballers and hustler's
But when you check they child support they really some busters
Rappers got the game messed up and everybody confused
You can't afford to ball all week and still buy your kids some shoes
If everyone would just stay in their lane a lot of the flossing would stop
Its okay to admit you got that dress from the thrift shop
Realize you don't have Jay Z and Beyonce cash
Stretch that check you know it has to last!

$\mathcal{T}$RUE TO THE ART

Open the door and let this lyricist slide through
Yall thought I was frilly and silly well now I'm about to clown you
All you so called rabbits with your tricks of voodoo
I aint from New Orleans but that shit is see through
The game has been infiltrated
I'm coming to let you know your rhymes are out dated
I'm bout to take you off the shelf
I don't need a stock crew I can do it myself
You chickens is lame all you do is complain
Even your names sound the same
Like Lil this and Young that
Ask Kim even she knows its whack
Let the real poets showcase rhymes
We been ripping the mic since the
Beginning of time
True to the art I
let my words reach the heart
You imposters come in trying to blend
You stand out like pencils
Amongst pens
Wanna be like us so bad
Sounding like Dr. Seuss better yet
Malibu Brad
Can't hold your own on the stage
Consider yourself a Wii cause you just
Got played
Never under estimate the power of a female

We will buy you then put you back up for sale
Don't come in the kitchen unless you ready to cook
Next time you think about battling stay in the crowd and
Just look

Grow

I say I'm ready for my flows to grow
but my flows can't begin to grow
until I step up and grow with them
forgot all inhibitions and get lifted.
Reach for higher heights in this thing that we call poetry.
Let my readers and listeners know that I am a grown up lyrically.
Stop talking about all the elementary tales of love fantasy.
Start giving people a dose of some real reality.
Some shit that you can spit when you realize he is a lie
and your man really aint shit.
See that's the lyrics I'm trying to get with.
Forget about romance
and proving that my words can stand alone without a stand
Release all my fears and dread.
Take off my tail and put on my head.
I was born to provide this art
I aint talking about a Picasso
I'm talking about the philosophical.
The rhymes that will play over and over again in your head
as you lie in your bed thinking about the way the world is fucked up
as upon God you begin to beg.
To open your eyes, remove the burdens that have happiness disguised.
Let me let go of this hate that I feel inside.
So that I can begin to rise and get lifted
so you can see that as a poet I am truly gifted.
So as I grow I want my lyrics to grow too.
Make my listeners know there is more to me than a hairdo.
I have something to spit
something more than some elementary shit.
These they kind of rhymes I'm trying to get with.

HE BAD

She wears many hats and puts on many faces
She can't help but be diverse she's been to many places
Her ambitions go further than the eye can see
In her presence is where they all want to be
She captures them with her brown eyes.
About her sweet lips they often do fantasize
Miss Upper Echelon is out of most of their leagues
True but she lets them play and make believe
They can daydream about having her in their life
It probably won't come to pass their credentials aren't concise
Miss White Linen needs someone highly qualified
When she acknowledges her needs they will quickly oblige
Not many come equipped to handle this type of dame
She is far from similar and nothing like the same
A female definitely in her own lane
If you piss her off she will break you and make change
Some consider themselves to be dimes or top notch
Compared to her game they look like hop scotch
You can't compare her to those that are average
Like window shopping you can look but can have it
To get with Ray you have to step correct
Don't speak unless you coming with a fat paycheck

BEAUTY UNDEFINED

So they say I'm the prettiest one of them all
With eye lashes long and curling
I make all the men fall
When I do my dancing and twirling

I keep my hair and nails done like a star
My wardrobe is full of the finest designs
I get stares and winks from near or far
In a room full of people the attention is all mine

It's been said that I resemble Vivian Leigh
I stare into the mirror in awe of my great features
But even on a good day she wasn't as pretty as me
On a busy sidewalk I'm approached by wife seekers

To be as attractive as I am should be a crime
Lock me up in handcuffs and throw away the key
I am a criminal of glamour undefined
Till the end of time there will never be another
beauty like me

DEPTH OF THE SOUL

Genuine eyes look deep
Helping hands dare reach
Ingenious minds think
Joyful givers reap
Kindred spirits speak
Longing hearts leap

THE TRUTH, THE WAY, AND THE LIGHT

No one said life would be easy as a matter a fact it can get quite hard
If we knew the ending why wouldn't we just show all our cards?
In life you have to learn from your own mistakes
Find the real people amongst all the fakes
Realize they will come into your life and pretend they're your friends
But behind your back their wolves in sheep's skin
I can't get over how they will stab you in the back
Steal from you when they see you with lack
The world at times will become awful cold
We walk everyday amongst devils without souls
They want to trap you and bring you down to their size
They will tarnish your life and leave you victimized
This is if you let them in and allow them to take control
Your best defense is to live a righteous life and stay in prayer mode
Jesus is the only truth in this world you will ever find
Let him into your heart and allow his gift to shine
Through your actions you can begin to set a trend
Show others there is no purpose for a life full of sin

Section 2

Road to Heartbreak

Can I Walk With You

Can I walk with you?
Would you like to know my name?
I'm so glad you let me talk to you
Your vibes are telling me the same
Can I walk with you?
Let me tell you who I am
I work across the street
I'm not a simple man
Can I walk with you?
I hate you're only here for awhile
Let me spend the day with you
I'm certain I can make you smile
Can I walk with you?
I don't want to keep you from eating
Let me get back over here
In a few minutes I hope you're not sleeping
Can I walk with you?
I told you I'd call in a few
Chilling with you is cool
So tonight what do you want to do?
Can I walk with you?
Hanging out was great but morning
Comes too fast
Can I walk with you?
I promise I'll make it last.

THE GAME

Jordan called the shot
Kobe caught the ball
Shaq missed the free throw
But you got the rebound

$\mathcal{B}$ULLET PROOF

I don't have to be pierced with a bullet to know what it feels like to internally bleed.
You sowed the hurt and now I am reaping from its seed.
I felt the sting even before you threw the blow.
Why you would want to hurt me I still don't know.
Through the circumstances I was trying to make you King.
From your actions I see I was not your idea of a Queen.
I was ready to make changes to bring you into my world.
But I guess to you I'm just another girl.
Your heart doesn't beat for me like mine does for you.
You don't lay awake in your bed wishing I was there too.
Why you led me on this entire time will remain a mystery.
My feelings for you will also go down in history.
Mere words will not place love for me in your heart.
On that note from this misery I shall depart.
With my bruised ego and aching chest, I will walk away with one last request.
Make sure the next lady you shoot has on a bullet proof vest!

Text Craze

I wake up in the morning and immediately
I turn on my cell and there is no icon that lets me know he was thinking of me
As I was dreaming of him
Still every hour on the hour I'm checking the display
Hoping that little envelope is there that lets me know I have a message.
Maybe it will say something sweet like "just saying hi" or "xoxo"
He could even go as far as to leave a numeric "143"
I would know exactly what he means
Unfortunately after lunch that little envelope still isn't there.
I turn the phone off praying that there is just a bad connection
And my messages aren't coming through
And that when I finally get the phone back on
Magically my favorite icon will appear
Letting me know that he loves me back
And I can relax from all this text message anxiety.
Coincidentally when I power
The phone back up I am not greeted by the envelope at all.
The only message I receive on the display is a missed call.
Even that wasn't him so I throw the phone in a fit of rage.
I have become consumed with this text message craze.

*M*ISSING

I beckoned and you and you never came
My sunshine quickly turned to rain
I stopped dreaming and wishing on stars
My heart beat on Venus and yours Mars
My calls never reached your ears
Your cheeks never felt these tears
Words could never capture the hurt
Enjambment and prose won't work
Only my eyes can reveal the pain
When you look into them are you ashamed
You abandoned me and left me alone
Neglect is something my heart can't condone
You were wrong and should apologize
Better yet just come home save the lies

A Year

It took you a year to break my heart in two
It took you a year to say "I don't love you"
Why couldn't I read between the lines?
You never wanted to be with me
For a year I lived a lie
Shame on you for not being a real man
Shame on you for not giving a damn
Yes a lot of the shame belongs to you
But as I reflect I can accept some of the blame too
I should have seen the end for us was drawing near
I should have known your words weren't sincere
Truth is you never gave me any words at all
Most of our conversations were frivolous brief calls
You never opened up your heart and let me inside
To my ears you never let your truths confide
For a year you wasted my money and my time
For a year you proved to not be worth a dime

$\mathscr{S}$ECRET LOVERS

The first day I laid eyes on you my mind was intrigued.
The sound of your voice made things move in me that
You wouldn't believe.
Immediately I was captivated by your smile
My initial desire was to have a conversation with you for awhile
For months I kept my secret desires inside
Until the day when my feelings I no longer wanted to hide
I wanted you to know you had my nose opened wide
So I let you know just what I was keeping in
You are now aware of how I want us to start and end
I'm no fool and I know your heart belongs to another
All I'm asking is if I can be your secret lover.

"*I* can be her"

You don't have to look any further because I'm right here
Open your eyes to all the possibilities let's make it clear
Whatever you thought you needed I'm here to provide
Welcome me into your heart let me come inside
Let me kiss you softly while I love you hard
Let me heel your wounds I see that your scared
I can nurture you and bring back your glow
Love you so much even the scars won't show
My touch can make you feel like silk
My embrace is like repentance it frees you of guilt
The door is never locked but you have the master key
Let down your guard allow me to love you compassionately
I'm not trying to steal you or hold you hostage
I just want to elevate you from all that bondage
I won't incarcerate you but you will be my prisoner
Obliged to receive my love like an Amish parishioner
If you ever envisioned or dreamed of being a King
Accept my offer; be loved by your Queen

GOT TILL IT'S GONE

As I sit and look at the way she treats you in public I get angry and want to slap her in her face
Doesn't she know that at the drop of a dime a million women would be willing to take her place
Oh if she doesn't she better grab a pen and take some notes
What she considers a burden someone is dying to tote
See it mesmerizes me that there are women who don't understand that they have a good man
Instead of complimenting him and praising him they curse and make demands
Like an obedient child I notice he quietly does everything that she asks
If I were him I would tell that sister to politely kiss my ass
She could never appreciate the inner man that she tries to chastise
Doesn't understand the importance or value of a compromise
It isn't until she finds herself alone that she begins to realize
No matter how bad she believed him to be there is always someone out there worse than he
She could have ended up with the dog who loves to bring home fleas
Or better yet the psychopath who loved to beat her down to her knees
I bet she would have worshipped the guy with the hazel eyes
Although he really wanted a man and women he despised
Only a fool tears down her house with her own hands
Instead of belittling him try uplifting your man

$\mathscr{D}$ear Wifey

Dear Rita my name is Kita
I was wondering if it was okay to meet cha
Sadly I think it's something you should know.
I've been sleeping with Keith, and no I'm not a hoe.
See things between Keith and I went really fast.
I thought it was a fling. I wasn't looking for anything to last.
But as you know Keith is one hell of a guy.
He really has my head gone and I can't even lie.
The way he touches me sends chills down my spine
His kisses I could never decline
Here I am at a crossword so to speak
Keep up my affair or from Keith retreat
Logic says what we have isn't love at all.
From me all Keith wants is a booty call.
It really isn't a disappointment to me though.
Seeing the way this panes out is helping me to grow.
I get a firsthand look at men like Keith.
It lets me know that Cheaters will always cheat.
Because even if I decided to tell him no.
Good old Keith would just move on to the next hoe.
Unfortunately you are the only one hurt in this equation.
You never knew your husband had the gift of persuasion.
So for now all I ask is that you can see it from my point of view.
I wasn't trying to steal I just borrowed Keith from you

RAPPED

Captive in this jail that holds no happy endings
Quarrels and headaches are many
These walls do not see smiles or witness
Hugs that reconcile
Angry and bitter tales are forever told
No winning hands were dealt it's time to fold
Victims of our own selfishness
We've become subdued and helpless
No one wants to make the first move
But we need to admit the story is ready
To conclude
The climax has been reached and we are
Ready to descend
Let's call it quits while we can still be friends
I don't want to hate you and I hope you understand
Being in a loveless relationship is like
Being trapped in quicksand
The longer I stay the harder it is to breath
I'm not ready to die so it's best that I leave
Parting will benefit you as well as I
Once you read this Dear John there's
No need to reply

Soon

My voice falls on deaf ears,
I shed unnoticed tears.
I live a life consumed with regret.
I harbor a love that suffers from neglect.
I hold feelings in my heart for him that are offered in vain.
I can't understand why for me he doesn't feel the same.
Am I not worthy of his love and devotion?
Would loving me cause too much of a commotion?
For him I would navigate the seven seas.
If only in my love he would just believe.
Love isn't always in the package that we choose.
Sometimes that package is full of heartache and blues.
I may not be shiny and wrapped in a bow,
but love in my heart for him continues to grow.
He may not notice me or give my love a chance.
But because God said so we will end in romance.
I knew from the day we met that he would be my everlasting.
Like the color purple it's hard to notice my love and keep on passing.

COME FOR ME

As I awaken from a restless night I weep for the love that which I have never
known
He has never come for me to take me away into his chambers
Where he would lavish me with love from a pure and sincere heart
There he would have protected me from the dangerous and hurtful
men that were sure to capture me and use me for their own selfish
pleasures
But yet for his presence I still wait up for day in and day out
Never finding peace in his arms, never knowing the gifts of his heart
My love oh sweet love why have you not come for me
Can you not hear how loud my heart calls for you
Can you not feel the burn of my tears as I weep for you in my dreams
Dreams that will never come to exist because you can't see the
inner soul of me
The vision of my undying love for you is not yet clear to your naked eye
It is true blindness that leaves you in darkness and it is my love,
true love that could lead you into the light
Without each other's love we will surely perish never knowing the reality of
being in love
How sad that day will be if I awaken to my death and you have yet to come
for me

$\mathcal{C}$HASING FAIRYTALES

Looking in your eyes the truth hurts more than a lie
I can't see the depth that I want to see
At home the gaze I'm looking for is staring back at me
Trying to grasp at a mirage has had me chasing an infinite dream
Something that will never come true I hold on tow what it seems
The reality of it though is what I yearn for may never be
I desire a fairytale love affair
When I reflect on past relationships that feeling was never there
Are my expectations too high?
While waiting on Prince Charming am I living a lie?
Should I just open my heart to what is already there?
Or keep dreaming and pray that he is out there somewhere
In the meantime while I sift through these thoughts
I will travel in the moment and hope in love I get lost

FADED PICTURES

Alone, she lay awake in her bed
The quiet sound of the wind whispering its good nights to the moon
The day had made promises to her that were broken like
Shattered bar room glass
Her expectations had gotten lost somewhere on Route 66
As she began to close her eyes only visions of his arms
Wrapped around her could be seen
Her face in the vision was one she couldn't recognize
It held a smile that told everyone looking on that she
Had finally found the man of her dreams
Underneath her warm blankets she smiled at her
Twin in the vision
Although they were fraternal she hoped one day
Her features would be identical to the women she
Peered at through tight shut eyes
She desired to be the exact replica of the lady
Who had found her Prince Charming amongst
All the Kermit the Frogs of the world
As she drifted off to a deep sleep she ran into
Her twin and her Prince Charming lying in a field of daffodils
He lay underneath her stroking her hair and kissing her ever so softly
The scene was beautiful and sad all at the same time
The picture displayed was a reenactment of days gone by
It wasn't a vision of a life yet to be lived
She was getting a glimpse of a love that had slowly slipped away

$\mathcal{L}$ONELY SONG

She sings her soul out every night hoping that he hears
In the shadows he listens contemplating his fears
Should he let her know that he feels her vocals?
Or should he stay in the dark and pretend to be a local
He wants so bad to grab her by her waist
Let her stanzas dry the tears from his face
But he never lets her see him or know that he's there
Sadly she croons hoping the lyrics find him somewhere
In a passionate tune she relays to the audience her pain
Her falsettos help to create artful tear drop stains
In the dark he admires her range and tones
He gets enveloped in her silent pheromones
Frustrated and agitated every night they journey home
To lonely beds and frequent dreads they sleep alone
In their dreams they stop playing the crushing game
They look into each other's eyes and erase the pain
For the first time he joins in creating a duet
The creation is a song that hasn't ended yet

Section 3

New Beginnings

Next Time

So many came with intentions of breaking my heart
But they never mention that to me.
They just crept on in and laid their burdens down
And I like the clown
Picked them up and tried to be the bearer that
They needed
Verbally I never pleaded
That there was something that I lacked
I waited on them to notice and then to react
I needed attention and caring and
Obviously this was something they never
Thought about sharing
They were in it to get what they could get
Drain the well dry and spend up every cent
Ignore my wishes and overlook my desires
Leave me unsatisfied taking cold showers
Like a fool I stayed and to the Lord I prayed
Seeking the courage to stand up and shout
That love is what I needed and the next
Brother who comes along better be it

*L*OVE

Let us go back to the days of true love
when you knew it was love
and u embraced love
Lets go back to the days when you tried to save love
never throwing away love.
I want to go back to the day when you didn't have to buy love
and love gave love
and it was never just a take love
when you could smell love
and u wanted to taste love
and you heard love and felt love.
Back when it was easy to love
and you weren't scared of love
never ran away from love
cause it was that real love
not artificial superficial love.
Do you remember that innocent puppy love
no shame love
meet my parents love
share my last name love.
Well I remember and
I want to relive that same love.

UNCONDITIONALLY

To you I give my heart unconditionally
You are more than I ever expected you to be
I don't require you to change who you are
You don't have to drive the fanciest car
For me to value your true identity
I still love you unconditionally

You don't have to buy me expensive gifts
For me to place my heart in your hands
I don't require empty promises just someone
Who I know loves me and understands
I know you won't always go willingly
But I still love you unconditionally

If you lost your job and had nothing to give
I would still be there for you
What's mine is yours and what's yours is mine
If you searched into my heart it's sincerity you
Would find
My desires go far beyond what the eyes can see
That's why I will always love you unconditionally.

ISSES

Keep your eyes closed, open up wide
Let my tongue enter your mouth
Release your inhibitions with pride
Don't hold back, let love soar
Take your walls down
Allow me to kiss you some more
All I want is to lead, so follow my trail
Let's overcome all obstacles
Emotions over circumstances will prevail
Give me the moment, all I need is time
Forget about the clock
Stolen moments are surely divine
Consider the cause, appreciate the effect
Get lost in my love
Hold on don't let go yet
Share just one more stroke, another embrace
Look into my eyes
Let my kiss plead my case
I'm guilty of it all, throw away the key
Your heart belongs to her
Your mind will stay on me!

$\mathcal{I}$NDESCRIBABLE

If I had to call it, I might yell Infatuation!
If I had to write it I might use alliteration.
If I had to present you to an audience, it would be befitting.
I'd use a PowerPoint presentation, something strong and uplifting.
High above the clouds and far from the Earth.
When I look into your eyes they reflect my true worth.
If I had to measure my love I would use kiloliters.
The joy that fills my heart couldn't be any sweeter.
You're that taste that I constantly crave.
Memories of you are the sugar to my salty days.
Passion, intensity, luster, felicity,
Are just some of the words you bring to me.
The depth of my feelings you can always seek.
Truthfully you will never get there, that distance can't be reached.
You can try to understand it, even Google the definition.
Sadly no search engine known to man is that omniscient.
From my words I hope you can see through the windowpane
That my love is incomprehensible, yet easy to sustain.
It shall never falter or from its path waver.
In my heart it dwells in an indestructible container.

HEAT

My thoughts play like a song
I tap my feet and begin to sing along
The tune is beautiful and the hook is nice
All I need is a margarita on some ice
The lyrics promise passion and bliss
I lick my lips and can taste our first kiss
Your mouth was delicious like sweet mangos
Our tongues got lost in a lovers tango
As the beat goes on I can hear my heart pound
My mind is racing, mimicking the sound
I dance in my seat feeling the groove
Internal urges cry out to be soothed
Only your hips and dips can accomplish the task
You're the only once can bring it and make it last
Before the song ends on my phone I press send
Hopefully when I reach you I can cum again

$\mathcal{F}$ORMAL PROPOSAL

I present to you this formal proposal,
It's one you can choose to decline.
An answer isn't needed today,
By all means take your time.
I don't want you rushing into this,
Without letting it weigh on your mind.
Decisions of this magnitude should
Be thought about,
Hastiness leads to the road of demise.
There is no room for errors,
Be sure you can easily deal.
Once the terms are granted,
The contract will be sealed.
With a yes your fate lies in my hands,
A no will leave the offer where it stands.
There will be no do overs,
Or let me try it again.
Be sure you are ready,
None of these stipulations shall I rescind.
With me it's all or nothing,
Take it or leave it.
This proposal is guaranteed.
Yes baby believe it!

In Disguise

Hey Love, can I ask for a moment of your time?
Let me paint this picture while the pleasures all mine.
Let my words captivate you and let my feelings seep through.
I'm not here to astound but I want to arouse you.
I want my words to embrace your soul.
I want these lyrics to make your body shiver, and your mind lose control.
With each word I want your heart to skip a beat.
I want to turn my love into a song so you can put it on repeat.
Throughout the day I want you to visualize my touch.
I want you to itch from the feeling of wanting me so much.
Can you fantasize about the way it feels between my thighs?
Does the image of my silhouette cause your nature to rise?
If you can suffer through the pain the end is such a surprise.
If I said I wasn't wet right now my mouth would be full of lies.
Because we can't be too forward I'll use this poem as my sex in disguise.

$\mathcal{H}$idden in Plain Sight

Be cool don't stare too long
it may become obvious that there is more than a casual connection
between you and I.
Our secret may become exposed if I let my eyes linger too long on your face
and then it will be apparent that my heart skipped a beat
when I allow my gaze to drift downwards
and then upwards once more,
I hope no one saw the way my lips curled up at the corners
as the memories came rushing back
So intense was the recollection that I had to put my head in my hands
because there was no way that the images were not playing on my pupils
giving the rest of our audience a glimpse into our encounters.
Surely we couldn't explain why we were conjoined at the hips
in a sensual manner that mimicked a Latino salsa
where you would lead and I would follow to the tune of our beating hearts.
Nope we can't let that scene replay
because if they knew the things that we did in privacy
they definitely would not understand.
They couldn't relate to the natural attraction that draws me nearer to you
and you to I
so strong that even in good sense we ignore warning and caution signs
as we travel at top speed down a slippery slope that ends with our bodies
intertwined
and our hearts racing to reach the same finish line.
For the safety of the innocent let's keep the fire between us dim
and never let the spark show
This is a secret no one can ever know!

ANTASY

I feel it deep within my being
A feeling you can describe without seeing
The tingle lasts all day and night
These sudden urges I don't want to fight
I think back to our first kiss when you took me by surprise
When it was over I thought I hadn't opened my eyes
For a moment I was blinded by the passion
You tongue danced with me and inside something happened
From that day forward my mind replays the moment like it's
On constant repeat
And I fantasize about the two of us playing hide and go seek
I will get undressed from head to toe and let you take a peak
There are no rules so whatever you desire I'm at your request
I promise to give you my all and nothing less
For one night you can make my fantasy a reality
Just come along for the ride and let me take the lead

$\mathcal{T}$HE MORNING AFTER

A door that opens after being shut for so long
I walk in and immediately I feel like I'm home
The surroundings seem familiar and I can reminisce
On the first day we met I remember our first kiss
That night you took my whole body in
We talked for hours just like old time friends
I felt no pressure and you applied no pain
Your presence was a ray of sunshine after nonstop rain
There were no words that needed to be said
I wanted to be pleased and down that rode you lead
Without GPS we found our way to ecstasy
The next morning I found you lying next to me
Although our journey could only be a one night trip
I never let you leave my life to you I held a tight grip
It was obvious I had found someone in tune with my needs
To get my desires I didn't have to beg or plead
So here we are again standing at this crossroad
Do I turn away or let my body explode
Let's not deny each other a night of fun and laughter
The feeling is so good the morning after

$\mathcal{S}$ECRET PARADISE

Secluded in the forbidden gardens that only we know exist, we escape to a paradise that promises internal and external bliss.

Tucked away far from any form of creation we invite each other to live out those fantasies that have been denied for so long.

Here in our secret place there doesn't stand a chance that our intimate embraces will be interrupted by unwanted intruders.

I get the chance to indulge myself with warm conversations, followed by hot kisses that lead to heavy breathing and low moans.

Far from any listening ears yet I whisper the sweet longings that live in my heart.

With every word you realize that this journey was more about the after than the now.

Without the love making you sense the love that permeates from my pores for you.

In this special moment I want you to realize that I'm tired of harboring my feelings for you, carrying them around like a heavy weight in my chest.

My thrusts let you know that I am ready to release all of this caged love onto you.

After this day I don't want my love to be a secret anymore.

I want to leave the secrets in this garden with the evidence of this forbidden excursion.

On my skin I want you to paint the love that you have for me in long strokes that tell the stories beginning but you can leave off the end because like this moment I hope it never ends.

Etch the inner thoughts that you have for me on every inch of my being that way even when you're not around I will know the words are there.

Inscribe your love on my heart and let the world know that what we both feel is real.
Don't allow my fantasies to only come true tucked away in a secluded garden that is forbidden, I'm tired of painting love on a canvas that no one will ever see.

*E*NOUGH

The greatest task is putting to words the emotions felt by the heart.
It's easier to give the ending but hard to capture the start
Love is an emotion that sweeps through like a tidal wave
You may not remember the moment but you sure know the day
As love begins to wrap you in its strong embrace
Thoughts and longings becoming impossible to shake
Similar to the effects of an asthma attack
Love takes your breath away and makes it hard to react
Once you have been consumed by the need to give all of you
A million words, hugs, nor kisses could ever do
The picture for how you feel could never be beautiful enough
You would travel to the ends of the earth no matter how tough
If the stars were yours you would lay them at their side
Undying affection you would never try to hide
Their presence would paint a permanent smile on your face
It becomes a blessing just to be able to share that person's space
You can put money on it as all of these words before you are true
So are my feelings and I could never fully express how much I love you

EWIND

Words where have you gone as I decide to write down these lyrics of how he made me feel.

It is so easy to go over the metaphors in my mind all the while pressing rewind on the play button that reminds me of the moments we shared, wrapped in a strong embrace as he nibbled on my neck and as I stroked the side of his face. But now as I try to embark on that passage of ecstasy again the words don't seem to flow the way I would like them to. I want to paint vivid pictures with similes and analogies so that maybe I can capture the creativity of the kiss that he gave that set my soul on fire and even at this moment has my heart beginning to race. No comparison could bring life to the passion that we shared in those stolen moments when all was silent, when all you could hear were soft moans and an occasional gasp. Not even the most expensive GPS could get me back to those moments when for the first time in a long time I was floating on air. Not afraid of the fall because I knew he was right there. How do you explain bliss that was so intoxicating that it would put all drugs to shame, for this obstacle of mine he is to blame? At his hands I have experienced something too intense to fully describe. For that reason I will put the keyboard aside. For this occasion I will just hop on Memory Lane and take a ride.

Section 4

Same Endings

BOSTON

Across the bay I look at you and awe in your beauty.
Your magnificent history captivates me.
I could stare at your scenery for hours on end
And never tire from the view
Every imperfection you possess is perfected in my eyes
I cast no judgment on you for it is only greatness that I see
Gazing at the night skies I wish upon listening stars that
We might meet again
That I might wake up to your morning glow and slumber
In your delicate embrace
Yet invisible gates surround you with silent authority
A shield I dare not attempt to break through
Intuition lets me know the limitations of my entry
With wisdom I stand in the shadows admiring
I'm forced to look at you from a far and only hope
One day I would be allowed entry into those gates
Where I know I would dwell in complete contentment
There no hunger shall go malnourished
And all thirsts shall be quenched.
All dreams will manifest themselves into realities
Memories of you will forever be cherished until we meet again
Boston you are a long lost lover, Boston you are an endearing friend

$\mathcal{I}$NCOMPLETE

The company isn't the same
Vivid memories remain
The experience is different
The feelings something new
I saw a movie theater and it
Reminded me of you
The emptiness won't go away
I reach for your arm yet
You're too far away
Distance is harsh and reality cold
We quit too soon the story was
Never told
The abruptness of your departure
Leaves me stunned
You left the game before it started
To get fun
Why don't you come back and see
Who wins?
I promise to let you if only we could
Play again

FYI

As senseless as a head with no brain
As dry as a desert without rain
As pure as a heart that never felt pain
I love you openly without a trace of shame
I would write it across the sky
I would bellow it out if asked why
I would carry us if I had to
There is no doubt I'm head over heels for you
My mind won't let me sleep
I think about you seven days a week
I'm at a Summit without a peak
Without you in my life my days are bleak
I wanna shower you with gifts
I wanna lay in your arms and drift
I wanna hold and console you
I thank the Gods who helped to mold you
Your voice soothes my soul
Your smile is warming when I'm cold
Your kisses are soft and sweet
You're the half that makes me complete
I wanted you to understand exactly how I felt
I wanted this to heat you and make your heart melt
If I have accomplished anything I hope that it's this
I have to thank my Genie because he has truly granted my wish

$\mathscr{Y}$ou

What is it about you that make me want to breathe the same air you breathe?
Drink from the same cup as you
Share the same meals with you
cry the same tears as you
I want to laugh from the same jokes as you.
I want to heal from the same pain as you
Wish on the same stars as you
I yearn to have an orgasm at the same time as you
Can I be at one with you
Can I hold your hand and pray the same prayers as you.
I already know I worship the same God as you
I want to listen to the rain with you
Make love on the same sheets with you
Yes I love no other man but you
That's why I want to share a home with you
Pretend to make babies with you
I just want to lay with you
Wake up to the same sunshine as you
Laugh, smile, and cry with you
But most of all share the same name as you

ORN

Unattainable, un-claimable, everything I want in this world
Already taken, a love forsaken, I could never be your girl
I tried and you lied, but the truth is between the lines
A quick peek, days waiting to sneak, evidence left behind
Memories of secret conquests, burdens laid to rest, you make me feel warm inside
Lying awake, a chance I'm dying to take, many nights I've cried
Your finger bearing the ring, reality in the form of bling, it says everything I need to know
We could never be, your heart belongs to she, my mind says let it go
Still I come back for more, I guess my heart isn't sore, you're worth the pain
For moments of affection, I take part in life lessons, my love has me insane
I'm giving you my all; weeks go by without a call, a fool I choose to be
One day I will wake up, on that day I will have had enough
I'll forget about you and focus on me
But today is not the day; it's too strong I can't walk away
The way you touch my heart makes me want to stay

BLANK

A blank screen, a blank sheet of paper
everything blank except the back of my mind where all the memories of you
lay embedded.
I can't conjure up any words, not even the hateful ones I want to use in reference
to you. Instead of letting you know that I don't give a fuck about you
and you can go on with your life
and forget you ever met me,
all I want to write about is how bad I miss you
and question God why he won't send you back into my world.
Everything in me wants to tell you to kiss the entire circumference of my ass
but instead my pen decides it's better to write about how sweet your kisses
are
and how much I miss your lips pressed against my neck.
If I had my way I would drive pass your house and throw eggs at your
windows
but instead I type about how I wish I could cook you breakfast every morning
and bring it to you while you lie in bed.
It pisses me off that instead of deleting your number out of my phone
I write it down in my address book just in case I lose all the contacts in my
cell.
It's a damn shame that I started this poem with all the intentions of letting
you know that you don't have my heart
and I can move on from the point of thinking about you night and day
but the only words I could muster up say the exact opposite.

It's true I do give a fuck about you. So instead of fronting like you don't matter at all
I will leave the screen blank and the paper blank,
because without you in my life everything is blank.

DROWNING

Others call themselves deep but have they ever fallen so deep in love that they drowned in its racing waters, or had to fight to get to the top so they could breathe.

I don't know if anyone has ever fell as deep in love as I have fallen for you because I know for a fact that I drowned a long time ago and I haven't known what it feels like to breathe for quite some time.

See you came and took my breath away and made it hard for me to reach the surface.

But unlike most drowning victims I don't desire to fight the current.

It can take me away because I like not being able to escape your love.

I want to continue to let it cover and envelope me.

Kill all the things inside that aren't of love and kindness.

Let me drift in loves currents for as long as I live because to be carried back to shores would take away all my hope of finding this special kind of love again.

I have been so blessed to experience this type of feeling I wouldn't trade it for all the air in the world.

I'd rather die in love than live without it.

$\mathcal{I}$s It Over

I ask you could our love really be over.
Have you awaken from the dream and found yourself sober?
Have the effects of my addicting drug worn off?
Has our tab run out and I'm left with the cost?
Have you moved on to someone new?
Confirm my suspicion or give me a clue
While traveling down this highway have you decided to exit?
Did someone else capture your heart like I suspected?
How did I leave room for someone to walk in my shoes?
All these questions have left me tired and confused.
I want answers to the how and the why
Why did you leave me here without saying goodbye?
I at least deserve a confirmation email
That way on these questions I won't continue to dwell
It was my understanding we were right on course
Yet in still you abandoned me without an ounce of remorse
I'm standing here with pleading eyes asking for closure
Do you still have love for me or is it over?

"Expectations are for fools"

Let's take them down a notch
These unfulfilled expectations that I got
I don't want to assume the best
When I know I will get the worst
Help me to soften the blow
When I know it will hurt
It's ok for you to cushion my fall
Pretend that you love me when
You probably don't care at all
I can handle a lie better than the truth
Let me hold on to my hope
I don't want to cut it loose
Living in the shadows of make believe
Create more shade than any truth
You can conceive
I refuse to let insignificant
Details ruin the chances
Of true love being able to
Prevail
My mind is made up to ignore
Little known facts
If anyone comes near me
With truths they can
Just have them back
I like the masterpiece that
I have created.
I can't let reality cause me
To be jaded.

Expectations are for fools
I like to keep it breezy
And play it cool
So get away from me with that
Nonsense
I live in a fantasy and I
Like it.

Section 5

Moving Forward

LOVES RETREAT

Where is my shield from the heartaches of this cruel world?
There doesn't seem to be any solace available to this lonely girl.
I close my heart to the pain and hope that there will be some kind of sunshine
at the end of this rain.
How long must I cope and deal with this agony.
I want to open my mind and heart to all of the possibilities.
Can someone plant a seed that will grow a happy tree?
One that will provide shade from all this misery
For too many nights I've dreamed an impossible dream.
One where there is a ray of sunlight that exudes a radiant beam.
It lights my path and guides me to a special place.
Where I can let my hair down and let all fear is erased.
There I run through the rain and don't care about getting wet
I get to remove all thoughts of disappointment and regret
In my new place I let my heart be my guide
Renew my soul because long ago it died
Here I wrap myself up in garments of royalty
Only people devoted to treating me with loyalty
No more days of feeling agony and defeat
I'm moving on to my love retreat

.

OUNDATION

Like the foundation you build your house on your wife should be strong.
It's she who carries the weight of everyone within and around your home.
Although you are the head you need her to stay upright.
She is the confidant you need to talk to when things just aren't going right.
She will be there for you no matter what trial or tribulation may be at hand.
She is not just there to be needy and make demands.
Your wife you will know her when she crosses your path.
When you find love that is approved by Christ it can't help but to last.
Along the way you may experience turbulence and want to free yourself of stress.
But no relationship is strong unless it has been put to the test.
Because she deserves your love and admiration give her all that she needs.
In return she will be there to help you in your journey to succeed.
For no man is anything without a strong woman by his side.
When she has groomed him to her liking she can step back and look on with pride. Through him her strength shows and if he is weak it is because he did not have a sturdy foundation.
So look at the woman you are with deeply before you go about decision making.
Sometimes we are quick to make decisions that are not always wise.
When deciding on a wife or husband you should never compromise.
Don't settle for someone who is half of what you are looking for.
Wait a little while longer and seek the advise of God some more.

He will help you to notice the true soul-mate that he created with you in mind.

Never let getting married be a decision based on time.

Just like when deciding where you want to build your dream home.

Choose a wife with a background and foundation that is strong.

$\mathcal{G}$ood Thing

As he went about doing the work of God she appeared before his eyes
She knew him to be her Boaz and like Ruth she was a nice surprise
She stood before him and offered him her hand
She had been sent to meet him by the son of Man
As she spoke to him his soul filled with a new fire
For on that day he had met his true desire
To him she was a true beauty to behold
From the inside out in his presence she glowed
For she was good, fearfully, and wonderfully made
From the arms of her true Lover she had never strayed
She treated her body like her temple and it was neither
Worn nor tarnished
With her and for her the man could plant an abundant harvest
Together they would do the Lord's will
Throughout their days happiness and satisfaction they would always
Feel
With her strength she would uplift and encourage him
She would give unselfishly never putting her before them
That quality about her he would admire the most
She's never arrogant never quick to boast
She was complete all on her own
He had asked God for bread and she definitely wasn't stone
As he looked into her eyes and gave her his ring
He knew in his heart of hearts he had found a good thing.
Something New

I wanna be his main chick but he see me only as the same chick
The chick that all the niggas in the hood done been with
He can't see past what he thinks so he keeps me at arms length
I can't break through his wall he has built it out of concrete
I don't know if I should let it go or keep trying
My heart breaks everytime I think of where I wanna be
Haven't heard his voice in awhile wish that he would call me
Man I must be tripping this aint even like me
I always keep it gangsta with a least a side piece
But for some reason this dude got me vibing
I'm thinking about settling down and the sound of babies crying
He could be the one to take me out the game
I imagine signing my first with his last name
Yeah this is all new to me
Damn I must be crazy
Dude aint even my type
I never used to fall for the hype
But now my mind is made up
I guess that means he got me fucked up
He got my head gone and I like it
To my emotions I won't fight it
I hope he changes his mind
I'm tired of wasting time
He needs to come and wife me
Damn I'm tripping this aint even like me

HANGE

Confusion draped over my mind
Thoughts consumed by time
Shadows chase me from behind
Racing against the wind
My integrity I try to defend
Held captive by the tongues of men
Scrapping the walls I free my soul
Shield my heart from the cold
Transition my ways from the old
A brighter future is on the horizon
Above my childish ways I have wizened
My name in the clouds I see rising
No longer imprisoned by concern
Harm is now easily discerned
The right to happiness I have earned
Today I can walk into my promise
Dismissing the days of dishonest
Change is a reality I'm ready to encompass

$\mathcal{P}$ERFECT SENSE

Like pouring the water out of a fish tank
And expecting the fish to survive
Leaving me doesn't make sense
Like speeding down a steep hill knowing your
Brakes have just given out
Not loving me doesn't make sense
I can't get your mind to embrace
The fact that you belong in my arms
Every night allowing me to lay
This passionate love on you
Like a thick blanket you would
Cover up with on a cold winter's night
In Harlem.
Your eyes can't see the vision of our
Everlasting love so I provide you with
A bifocal that brings it all into focus
so that maybe just then you
Can begin to comprehend the essence
Of our union, and accept the truth
that it was
Predestined before you and I ever
Envisioned a love for ourselves.
We like fools could never know that
What was meant to be was far greater
Than any love we could have ever prayed for
Or hoped or dreamed for
In my mind the purpose has been made clear
And it is my job to get you to understand
That the only thing in life you must do
Is allow me to lavish you with love.
It's the only thing that makes
Perfect sense.

DESTINY

The way I feel is unconventional
What would be expected is defied
On every level of understanding
Two doesn't come after one
In the natural order of things
Up is not the top but somewhere
In between
Red doesn't mean stop but
Is just a slight caution
To proceed at a speed
We can handle
Soon is never too soon
And late means we won't
Wait
We can continue to go
With whatever flow soothes
Our urges
We can let our emotions
Take us where practicality is
Thrown to the wind
Forget what everyone thinks
And toss all opinions
In the trash cans of our
Minds

Destiny knocks only one
Time and I think
We should meet
Her at the door

OURNEY

Come with me on this journey that promises new beginnings and never ending nights of love making
that will leave your body shaking the morning after
when the breakfast is made and placed on the table for you to eat
to nourish your body so that you can go about your day
thinking about the love we made the evening before
when I called your name and beckoned you for more
Your nostrils will continue to carry the scent of me
making you hasten the clocks to reach quitting time
when I will again be yours and you will be mine.
Come on this journey with me and enjoy all that a life of true love has to offer
because for too long we have gone without each other
and we both deserve each other's love.
Not because we are perfect creatures but because we are imperfect apart
but together we are the perfect masterpiece.
Come on this journey with me when we forget all practicalities
and let our emotions drive us to our destinies and fantasies.
Take this ride that may not be smooth but at the end there is always a resting place.
There are no speed limits on this journey and there are definitely no stop signs.
Baby, come on this journey with me where I am yours and you are mine.
The road is one built on an incline.

Section 6

Dedications to Friends and Loved Ones

A Mission Complete

When you decided to embark on that new adventure in your life, you never knew it would have such an impact or cause your life so much strife.
You joined an organization that made all types of promises and told so many lies
Their agendas were never sincere oh they were quite contrived
So there you were a young man with many hopes and aspirations
You left home never knowing the battles you soon would be facing
They called you out to a mission four years ago today
A mission that would change your life in a major way
The hand you were dealt was one you did not ask for
After being crushed underneath that convoy they said you might not walk anymore
The devil thought he would get the glory for taking your life away
But the Lord had plans for you, so on this Earth you would stay
Yes many nights you would lie in that hospital bed
And yes you would be betrayed by the wife you chose to wed
But my God one day you were able to stand up on your own two feet
Victory was yours and now the true mission you could complete
Through your testimony you have the ability to touch someone's heart
In our Master's plan you are beginning to play your part.
He saved your life so that he could get the glory
Now hundreds and maybe thousands will come to hear you tell your story
As you stand and speak about the trials and tribulations you overcame
You provide inspiration so others can do the same
On April 24, 2004 God spoke and the Angels heard,
"Spare my child for I need him to preach my Word"

N Angel Calls

Coming into this world your birth was early and took everyone by surprise.
But you were welcomed with open arms, great love for you was in everyone's eyes.
As a child you were the captain that started the train to move.
Who would have imagined your sun set would come so soon.
Growing up you carried a spirit that few could understand.
As a young boy you took the role of a grown up man.
Always there for your siblings, the love you had for them obvious in every way.
You held no inhibitions; you always lived for the day.
Friends who knew you well can remember your humorous attitude towards life.
You never let things get to you, never burdened by strife.
A few years ago you were almost taken away.
Fortunately your life was spared; your family knew how to pray.
The world needed you for a little while longer, now the time has come.
The angels called your name; we need you to come with us.
Your work in the world is through.
God is waiting for you.
So knowing that his plan is not your own, Glenn, tell your family and friends not to weep.
In heaven with us is where you belong.

"FROM A FRIEND"

As a friend I offer my condolences as you begin to bereave.
The death of a loved one is so hard to believe.
I too can understand the pain that you feel.
The experience so sudden it doesn't seem real.
Although he was not one of my kin
I still looked at Henry as more than a friend
Very seldom do men like him cross your path
We shared the kind of friendship you want to last
True friends you don't have to call everyday
But when in you're in need they always know what to say
I will always cherish the memories we shared
Never a doubt in my mind I know that he cared
You too can hold on to the thoughts of good times
These thoughts can't be taken away they are yours and mine
With heavy hearts and minds we must carry on
Trust in God and know the pain won't last for long
Though the road to recovery will be rough
And at times you will have to break down and cry
Through the heartache and tears on God you must rely
Lean not to your own understanding
God is in control and doing the Master planning
This chapter of the book has ended but the story remains
Keep Henry in your hearts and I will do the same

Mr. Smart Mouth

I stand before you smiling to myself
Thinking damn that nigga is something else
You strutting cross the stage like you own that shit
The ladies standing at attention
Snapping they fingers and given applause
While I just stand in the corner thinking
Damn that nigga something else
I listen to your words and let your
Messages permeate my mind
Reflecting on your illustrations of time
Yet time stands still, my legs I can no longer feel
All I hear is the sound of your voice
Silk to my ears lace to my fingers
Your spoken rhythms beating against my heart
The melodies of intellect playing their part
I can't step out of the trance that has enveloped
My physical body, can't remove myself
From the mental fantasy that has you
Speaking those sensual words to me in my ear
I'm humming back to you "baby I can hear"
The groove you are putting on has to be specifically for
Me cause, everyone else in the room has disappeared
I never noticed when they left but now I can tell you myself
I think you should know, "nigga you something else"

OSITIVE

The venom that's running through your veins
is some powerful lethal shit that is a result of a lapse in thinking of the brain.
You opened the door to let this intruder in.
you didn't think about the consequences so now your health you can no longer defend
, having to take meds every four hours to keep the t-cells high.
Never imagined the words that he was spitting weren't anything but a lie.
You never recognized that he was running game.
Now you at the clinic every week wishing shit would change.
The reality is a harsh pill to swallow,
made yourself a victim because the crowd you wanted to follow.
Listening to your so called home girls telling you the niggas is caking and had you making your body available for sale.
Now you wish that new drug was on sale.
Wishing the results from that HIV test wasn't a fail.
Sadly those results can't turn into a negative,
he fucked you up and that's a positive
You can bet that you aren't the only one he had succumb to what you thought was fun,
playing Russian roulette with your life only difference the dick was the gun.
You pulled the trigger one too many times,
let him cum inside of you and leave his venom disguised.
Now the effects are being made crystal clear.
A baby isn't the only thing you fear.
You're dying a lonely death as a result of a positive test.

All of which could have been avoided if you wouldn't have allowed yourself
to be enticed by images of the fast life.
Now you are left to pay the ultimate price.
For a few dollars and a nut you paid with your life.
Moral of the story is keep it tight and if you just got to get it in,
make that dude strap twice.